Beauty Behind the Scars

Latisia Jones

Atlanta, GA

Latisia Jones
Atlanta, GA 30344
www.theeducatedbosschic.com

Publisher's Note: This is a work of nonfiction. Names, characters, places, and incidents are real.

Book Layout © 2017 BookDesignTemplates.com
Book Cover & Interior Design © Alexis M. Creative Agency LLC.

Beauty Behind the Scars/ Latisia Jones. -- 1st ed.
ISBN 978-0-578-77893--8

DEDICATION

To my sister in heaven, thank you for loving me always.

To my inspiration, my mother, thank you for your strength, your prayers, and grace under pressure.

To my spiritual parents, thank you for always believing in me and pushing me past my limits.

To my love, thank you for holding the ground and letting me fly.

To my tribe, each and every one of you are truly my vibe! I'm grateful to have such an amazing group of people on my team.

To the woman that is reading this, my prayer is that you are able to embrace every scar and recognize the beauty behind them all.

Contents

Goliath

IN 2002 I WAS DIAGNOSED WITH BREAST CANCER. As a wife and mother of two beautiful daughters, your mind immediately takes you through the worst-case scenario; What will life be like for my kids, my husband? Will I get to see my baby girl graduate college, watch my grandson grow up? Who will look after them if I'm gone? I wanted to do everything I could to be here for my family, so I did what the doctors told me to do; I had a lumpectomy, chemo, radiation and kept up with my yearly exams. During this time, my husband was on dialysis and he would go to his treatments, then come home and take care of me.

For seventeen years, there were no new developments in my health. For seventeen years life went on as usual; my eldest daughter was doing a fantastic job raising my grandson, my youngest daughter went on to graduate college and pursue her blooming career as an educator, life was good. Then 2013 happened. My husband, the man I loved for over 40 years passed. Though it was difficult his transition made the bond with my daughters stronger. For 17 years amidst life's ups and downs I was happy.

Then 2019 happens. I don't know about you, but the years that change your life are always the ones you remember the most or, they are the years you wish you could quickly forget.

I received a call to return to my doctor's office after my initial yearly exam to do a biopsy and to my dismay, cancer was found again, this time in my left breast. I decided it would be best to have a double mastectomy and in the course of making this decision, my eldest daughter suddenly passed away. No warning, no getting to say goodbye, nothing could prepare me for what life was about to take me through.

A month after burying my daughter and fighting to raise my only grandchild who was now motherless, I had the surgery with no complications, thank God. I only needed to take a pill daily and my recovery was swift. But five short months after surgery, my youngest daughter decides to have a mammogram for obvious reasons.

Her results were positive for cancer in her left breast and I was devastated. I didn't know what to think or believe; and to be honest, I blamed myself. I defeated this Goliath and now here it is again showing its ugly head in my daughter.

However, something happened during this process that I did not expect-I gained strength from her, even with her telling me she was the one gaining strength watching me. I realized the faith that she had from the moment she shared her diagnosis. She has that NOW faith- that Hebrews 11:1 kind of faith. She always says that faith without works is dead and every time things sound negative; I watch her put a positive spin on it and get back up again.

You may say this kind of faith is living in denial- you can't just "will" for something good to happen, that we must accept the cards we are dealt. But I am here to tell you as a widow, two-time cancer survivor, and a mother that buried her child, that you can have just a small amount of faith and watch it move mountains.

I am proud of my daughter for courageously sharing her story with you and letting the world know that yes, there is plenty to still be grateful for. We have the power of life and death in our tongues and as she says, "you can't say you have faith but turn around and say something negative- that ain't faith!" I can't take all the credit for having such an amazing child, she is God's child and I am so encouraged by who she is as a woman. I know you will enjoy hearing her story as I have enjoyed being her mother and you'll be able to tell your future generations yes- you can make it through anything!

Goliath Is Not Dead

JULY 22, 2020 GOLIATH SHOWED UP AGAIN. It was the middle of a blazing hot summer in Atlanta, GA. The noise of a typical urban African Braid Shop fills the room; The swing of the doors, soft music and gentle laughs rising from brown, melanin hands meticulously wrapping around locks of hair are stirring in the background. On a regular day, I am sitting in the chair of the main braider getting my braids undone, not knowing that everything about my life as an Atlanta educator, hopeless romantic, and woman of faith is about to drastically change.

I get the privilege of calling the Atlanta and Athens Georgia area home. Friend if you know anything about this part of the world you know you can count on crazy traffic, sports teams that keep you guessing, and living inside a big cultural melting pot of the world's brightest minds. I grew up with my sights set on attending college at Georgia State University, where I graduated and became a teacher in the Atlanta area school district.

Life was as normal as it could be for us as a small family; I had my mom, dad, big sister, and brother in love all surrounding me with the love and support I needed. My big sister got married young at nineteen just like my mom did, and would later make me a proud auntie of my only nephew.

While I was in college in the city, Goliath would show up in the form of my mother's first breast cancer diagnosis. I can remember not wanting to come home much because honestly, I just didn't want to see my mom like that and the fight my family had to endure. On top of this, my father as sick going back and forth to dialysis while taking care of my mom, but that is just the kind of man he was, he put his family first.

As life went on, my family would continue to suffer with health issues. In 2013 daddy's fight with renal failure would end, a blow that would strangely strengthen my family and pull us closer together. But nothing could prepare us for what the years 2019 and 2020 would bring.

Ring Ring! Startled, I see an unexpected phone call from my doctor. After my mom's second cancer scare in 2019, with seventeen years of her being cancer free, I went in December of 2019 to get a mammogram knowing that I could not take any chances with my health. The doctors would see a small lump, but never would confirm if it was cancerous or not. Then suddenly yesterday, months after December's visit, I was asked to get a biopsy done on my left breast.

Looking down at the phone and seeing my doctor's name should have been my first indication that something was terribly wrong. As his caring words rang in my ear, "Latisia, your biopsy was positive for cancer," I could do nothing but sit in the chair and try to keep my composure, afraid and alone.

Sitting in that braid shop with my stomach in knots, I was relieved when it was time for me to go twenty minutes later. I picked up the phone and called my boyfriend whose next words "So, what are our options? What's next?" assured me that somehow, everything would be okay. I knew Goliath was back, and I would have to fight.

****

Friend, this is where you and I pause and talk. If you are choosing to stick with me on this journey, I have to tell you something; This isn't a story with a cute before and after where I tell you that everything is going to be okay. No, I am going to tell you the truth that life can come at you fast and you really only have two choices; boss up and believe or lay down and die.

I don't know what your Goliath is, you know the unexpected giant that shows up in the middle of nowhere that no one is qualified to beat except you. Your Goliath doesn't have to be health issues, it can honestly be anything that attacks your faith and is leaving everyone around you scared to face it.

Maybe your Goliath is like mine, where you have seen more than your fair share of the inside of doctor's offices and hospital rooms, hoping that they would say something different. Maybe you have lost your greatest male example and have had to face storms without a dad. I don't know if you are still grieving the unexpected loss of one of your literal best friends in the form of a sister.

Oh yeah, I failed to mention that earlier. Just after my mom's second cancer diagnosis in 2019, we would suddenly lose my sister. No warning, no getting to say goodbye, no last laugh together, no nothing. My once vibrant family would go from shaken to shattered in a matter of weeks! Weeks!

Life doesn't necessarily give us a choice of what storms we will choose. If I could have chosen a storm to pick it certainly would not have been cancer for me or for my mom, abruptly losing my sister or losing my dad. I'm sure after all the things you have been through, you would not have chosen the path you are on either.

So why do we keep going? Why do we hear the yelling from Goliath in the valley wondering like David's brothers who is going to be the one to face it, when we know deep down inside the only person qualified to face it is us? You have been given everything you need to face your Goliath, even if it shows up again it is still your job to boss up and believe you can face it.

• CHAPTER 2 •

Goliath's Weapon: Fear

SHARING THIS JOURNEY IS INCREDIBLY VULNERABLE AND I FIND MYSELF CONSTANTLY FILLED WITH BITTER-SWEET EMOTIONS. I remember walking into the doctor's office in Marietta, around the corner and into the room with Dr. Rose. After sitting down and getting as comfortable as I could, I learned my cancer is has been caught in stage 1, meaning it is less than 2 centimeters and is not pressing on any major organs. However, I do have triple negative cancer which means that the hormone receptors that feed the growth of cancer cells (estrogen, her1 and her2) are negative; These cells are growing on their own. This cancer is stubborn and independent much like me. Selah.

I will also met with my oncologist for more testing to determine if the cancer has spread to other places in my body aside from my left breast. If my results are favorable, that means I can forgo chemo and take a pill for the rest of my life like my mother. That is the bitter news, but here comes the sweet; When I decided to randomly get that mammogram because of my mother's story, this was God saving me!

The reality is cancer can go undetected in the body for more than 80 percent of its life, with many people not finding out about the tumors until they are growing well into stage 3 or 4 and the cancer is pushing against major organs. Black women in particular have a higher rate of death from breast cancer than our white counterparts, for various reasons according to research by the American Cancer Society.

The most alarming is that is only 25% of us (women of color) have recently discussed our breast health with our friends, family, church members and colleagues and only 17% of us have taken steps to understand if we are even at risk for cancer[1]. Then there is the fact that so many persons of color do not have access to great health care to afford all the testing required due to the burden of financial cost[2].

Because of that by the time many of us know we are sick our cancer is well in its advanced stages, making it harder to treat. Also Triple Negative Breast Cancer, the kind that I just learned I have, doesn't respond very well to treatment and is more common in African American women[3].

Armed with the very real facts I cried with my boyfriend, cried in the doctor's office, cried by myself, with my spiritual mother and spiritual sister. However, those tears are in victory, praise and in gratefulness to God. I am grateful that he is mindful of me and for Him healing me already.

I am embracing the very real side of me that is human and afraid. I don't want the message of this book to get lost with you, celebrating the beauty behind your scars is choosing to fight *with* faith- not in denial of faith; It's choosing to know that the danger is very real and trusting God to shift things for you anyway. It's also choosing to allow people to be there for you, even when you are questioning your own existence. When we try to fight life's battles without anyone on our side, no family, no team, no church, no community that is when we really become weak. I have heard stories of cancer patients who choose not to tell their families. I am not here to judge anyone's journey, but I know that my support system is what has kept me motivated and alive.

Despite my diagnosis, I still believe God and I still trust that God has something BIG brewing. I don't know what's happening, I don't know how He is moving, and I don't know when or where the shift will start happening, but I believe I am already healed even though it is going to be difficult. God is still right here in the center of it and I am grateful. There is power of life and death in the tongue, so I speak life and I speak healing over my body. I know that God has created a purpose even in this storm and I trust him even the more. I thank Him for giving me the gift of faith, I thank for the strength he's given me to help others process.

CHAPTER 3

Cry it out

WHAT ARE YOUR CHOICES WHEN GOLIATH IS US-ING HIS NUMBER ONE WEAPON TO BULLY YOU? You may have to stop and ask yourself several times on your journey, why should I keep going? Who cares about my life and my jour-ney- do I really have a purpose?

Well before we can answer that, I want to tell you we have to do something- remove Goliath's number one weapon of choice fear. For God has not given us the spirit of fear, but of power and of love and of a sound mind. 2 Timothy 1:7 NKJV.

One thing we are taught is that f.e.a.r is nothing but false ev-idence appearing real. If you listen to the voice of fear long enough you will never make a decision. Your mind will tell you all sorts of things and you will even make yourself believe that if you died, no one would be bothered.

As I'm sitting at yet another doctor's appointment with my oncologist, a 20-minute drive from where I live, I must face the fear of making the wrong decision about my health. They are giving me all these options and honestly, a part of me wanted to glaze over and call my mom and cry, but I knew I couldn't I had to face the facts.

Let's just say we have the mastectomy and it removes the breast cancer- good right? The concern is if with just a tiny microorganism the cancer can shift to some other part of my body that the doctors can't find. Their solution is to give me an aggressive chemotherapy on top of the mastectomy to kill it. The challenge with chemo is of course the side effects.

One of the biggest side effects that I am concerned about is how it attacks my ovaries. I am not a mother yet and I am looking forward to motherhood. I have a lot of little people that I love to nurture and love on, but none of my own womb. Of course, I learned that I could not breast feed and that was a blow I got over quickly, but to have complications becoming pregnant- is something I am praying will not happen; this is not something I'm willing to accept as God's plan for me.

So, option one we have pre-op chemo do it and if the cancer responds well, I won't have to do a mastectomy. Second is post-op chemo for sixteen weeks and with chemo of course comes a lowered immune system, hair loss, fatigue etc.; I will go into a post-menopausal state where they will put my ovaries to sleep for 16 weeks (about 3 and a half months) and then 'wake them back up.' I was encouraged to do genetic testing as well as fertility with a reproductive specialist.

Finally, there is another option which is to do the surgery and the breast cancer is gone. If I don't do chemo, I risk this thing finding its way back in a year, 3 years, 5 years. The likelihood of that is about 20 percent, with chemo the likelihood is about 0.01% or 1 in 100 chances.

We have the facts but then we got faith. LET'S TALK FAITH. Faith says don't do chemo. My faith says this is your opportunity to walk it out and show how much you trust God. Trust that surgery will go well. Trust that there is no way His word will return void. Trust that anything that jeopardizes my ability to be a mother isn't for me. Trust that there will be no trace of cancer anywhere else in my body. That that will be all that I need, just trust God, breast cancer is gone and that is it. I'll be able to work on recovery and complete reconstruction with no hiccups. That's a faith move, a big faith move. I'll have to be closely monitored for years, but I trust God so much. A fear move would be listening to the doctors who say, "Hey, the numbers are okay but let's still go ahead and do the chemo." That would be moving by the facts which is really moving with fear.

As you could imagine, hearing all of this has been very overwhelming. Just a week after my initial diagnosis, I am grasping what it means to be a cancer patient in the present and how treatment options could be a future threat to my reproductive system and unborn children.

I've spoken with my boyfriend, my mom and my spiritual parents and I have some decisions to make. I'll be spending some time with God, talking with God, praying to God even the more, just to guide me. For now, the plan is to move forward with the surgery. God isn't telling me not to do that, so I have decided to forge forward with a double mastectomy. Some might call it dramatic, but I want to make sure that there is no chance this sickness can rear its ugly head again in my life.

****

Here is something I want to tell you, managing how people react to your news will be half of your process of facing fear. I am learning so many things about what it means to allow people to serve you and really be there for you when you are at your weakest, but also how not to allow other people's reactions to shake my faith.

I shared my cancer diagnosis with a few members of my church and honestly, I don't know how to say it. Like, how do you tell someone "Hey, I have cancer?" As I shared with my spiritual family, their reactions touched me in that I know that they care. Of course, I have always known that they care, but something as heavy as potential death can make people truly say anything to you. It's not just your faith you have to guard, but you also have to guard your heart!

I jumped on the phone recently to tell one of my dearest friends her response was, "I didn't want this for you," and that showed me her heart on a different level. I didn't want this for me either. I am happy that I have some amazing people around me to help me keep going for this battle ahead.

My biggest obstacle was telling my mother. I knew she didn't deserve to find out over the phone, so I made sure to sit her down and tell her in person. Her tears were endless as we processed together what felt like déjà vu for our family. I hated that she felt responsible for my cancer. We know that in black families the likelihood of cancer being genetic is very high.

I am clearly still processing all of this and crying tears filled with the signal that damn, life has officially changed for me. They're tears of sadness because my sister won't be here to hold my hand through the process, tears that verify that I am a human and it's okay to feel this is pain escaping my body. Because the truth is, I have a battle ahead. And my daddy ain't raise no punk. My family bloodline is strong and my spiritual bloodline is even stronger so, I am not crying these tears because I am sad, but because I am truly grateful.

My friend in case you were wondering, it's okay to feel. Don't let anyone tell you different. The one thing in my faith that I am reminded of is that Jesus lived his life as a human being. He lived inside of human body that is subject to suffering, pain, trauma, and weakness. He chose dying on the cross to let us all know that in weakness we find strength. He cares about our stories.

Knowing that I am cared for and loved by my heavenly father means that I have all the protection I need to get through this process and so do you.

CHAPTER 4

Roots & Relationships

IN ORDER TO CELEBRATE THE BEAUTY BEHIND YOUR SCARS, WE FIRST HAVE TO TALK ABOUT HOW THE SCARS GOT THERE IN THE FIRST PLACE. Our stories can leave some pretty painful places where life has cut us deeply.

According to the Merriam Webster Dictionary, the first definition of a scar is as a noun is, "A mark remaining (as on the skin) after injured tissue has healed." After my breast cancer surgery, I will have multiple scars on my once beautiful double d's but who cares.

These scars will remind me that I survived, these scars will remind me that I made it through my life darkest days, these scars tell the story that again, cancer messed with the wrong chic!

These scars bear the story that God has won again and that nothing by any means is impossible for him.

The second definition of having a scar that I found to be really interesting is, "A mark left where something was previously attached; a mark left on a stem or branch where a leaf or fruit has separated." Now these scars mean that something was once there that isn't there anymore and separation had to happen- like in our relationships.

The relationships we have can be compared to life on a tree; we have our roots, branches, and leaves. Our roots are the people who hold us down and keep us steady. They provide the nourishment that we need in life to keep us healthy, vibrant, and strong. We don't really lose our roots- as a matter of fact just like trees, you can only grow as high as your roots are deep. Normally if a tree is 6ft high, the roots are 6ft beneath the ground. If you want to grow and go far in life friend, you must have deeply rooted people to help you embrace the scars life will bring.

I am grateful for the support of my roots. Spiritually, emotionally, physically I know I got some praying people praying for me because I feel it. Physically I know there are so many people that won't let me fall and emotionally I can't even begin to describe because the emotional support has been unreal. I cannot help but to feel immense gratitude for the level of support that I feel, even from my doctors.

My mother is one of my roots who encourages me and gives me a perspective to love my scars. My mom has prayed for me and she spoke so much life over me and when I was making my choice for my surgery or doing chemo she said, "Whatever you do I support you." When my mom first emerged from her mastectomy surgery, her chest was completely flat. I remember her saying after surgery, "I'm not going to look," and she didn't. When I was deciding if I was going to look at my chest immediately after my surgery, I knew that I had to face it. I first looked at my scars post-surgery and honestly, I was so sad. My mom was like, "It's okay you're still beautiful," and that reassurance from my mom was everything to me.

One of my other roots is my boyfriend who is keeping me anchored in this process. In the three years that we've been together I have always said he holds the ground and lets me fly. This recent hurdle has been no different. Our love for each other is deep, but I wondered after the surgery and with talking with my therapist if he would think I am not beautiful anymore, which I know is insane. If anything, our love for each other has grown deeper.

We have talked about kids and with the threat of the chemo and all of these surgeries it might be hard to for us to get pregnant in the future. In one of our many talks he said, "We'll talk about kids later we just need you here. Whatever you do I'm with you." This type of encouragement let me know he is for sure with me and that I have nothing to fear. I am so grateful for the support I have from my mother, him, and my church family.

On my last Sunday physically in the building before surgery, I spent the day with my spiritual leaders. I was able to sit at the table and enjoy a meal prepared with love and it was amazing. We shared memories, laughs, tears; it was really food for my soul. My spiritual mother reminded me of who I am and it is with that message that I took with me throughout this process. She said, "This giant has already been defeated, my mother had already cut the head off of this Goliath and often giants will come back." Now it's time for me to cut the head off too!

The battle has already been won. My mama defeated this once before. So why can't I?! I cannot allow this thing to get me, because I know this battle is ninety percent mental. One hundred percent of this is all God and I know I have victory in him. So, I have to keep believing it and keep feeding my faith and not my fear. So that's what I am doing and that is how I'm preparing for my surgery by feeding my faith.

• CHAPTER 5 •

Branches and Leaves

Another group of people we will find out we have during our storms are our branches, the people we can depend on, but they are not our roots. If we step out too heavy on someone who isn't strong enough to carry our weight, that branch can break under the pressure. Once again though, God has proven to me during this storm that I don't have very many people I can't depend on, in fact, the support has been very overwhelming.

I found out my school is one of my amazing branches and I love how they have rallied around me. My principal held a meeting just to rally the support around me that I need for my process. He said, "Ms. Jones I just need you to work as much as you can leading up to your surgery and the rest we got." I cried like a baby, just to feel that level of love and support. One of my fellow teachers asked that I give her my food likes for my meal train which I never heard of before and I cried, just to know that people genuinely cared.

You will find in life though that perhaps most people in our lives that we come across are like the leaves on trees; they look beautiful, they provide some shade and shelter, but eventually their time to fall will come and they will wither away. Leaves in our lives are not mean to be permanent people.

When we confuse our roots with our branches, you know the people who love us unconditionally versus the people who aren't truly strong enough to carry us, that is when life can get complicated. Your tribe is your vibe and you really do have to fight to keep the right people around you and know who you can depend on. So how do you tell your roots from your branches? One word.

Storms.

That's right, there is nothing like a storm to come in your life that will expose weak branches and leaves. Living in the south we get some really terrible spring storms along with tornadoes, and heck even damage from hurricanes. After every single storm, you can count on walking out in the street and seeing broken branches and leaves all over the ground. But rarely will you see a tree with exposed roots, unless that tree was just really old.

When the branches in our lives break, it leaves scars because we were attached to those people. When the storms come and reveal who we could not trust, it can hurt us and leave scars. Celebrating the beauty behind the scars left by people separating from us simply means knowing their season was up and we have carried them far enough.

You might be carrying the scars of significant others who have left, the pain from a divorce, or friends who are no longer there. Whatever the case, you have to grieve the people who are no longer there and have left their scars.

I am finding out during my present storm that some people simply don't know how to handle your news, and some just don't take the time to think about how their words and actions can impact you. Also, you really do have to be careful how you tell people about your storms because some people simply love you deeply and grieve with you.

My best friend up over 20 years recently had a birthday and I couldn't tell her about my cancer news on her big day, because I didn't want to make the moment about me. I told her the next day and she cried, I cried, and it was once again a lot of tears. As I was trying to process everything, I learned that we have to give other people their opportunity process and give them the space that they need.

During this time, I also had another friend to call me and dump her relationship stuff on me-it didn't dawn on her first to ask how I was doing but eventually she did. This conversation was refreshing because I was just her friend and she was mine. I didn't have to talk about being sick, I got to be normal person. Cancer didn't matter. It didn't change our relationship and it didn't dominate the conversation, we were just two friends laughing and fussing about relationships.

Some people no matter how close they are to us process it (hard news) completely different from other people and we have to give those people an opportunity to grieve for us. I am thankful for my amazing friends and I know that as they have interceded on my behalf, that God will give them those things that they've been asking for, even secret things that they've laid before God.

But can I be honest? I don't want to always talk about cancer! I don't want to talk about it every time I talk to people because that's a portion of who I am, but this is not all of who I am. I spoke with a couple people recently and they were like "Hey... how ya doing?" I could hear it in their tone that they were sad, and I took authority and immediately told them, "I'm good!" in the most cheerful and steady voice I could find. Of course, their words were, "I'm praying for you," and I was like "Specific prayers? Don't just pray, be specific! Don't pray willie nillie I need specific prayers!" It felt good to boss it- to tell people and their words what to do and where to go.

Oftentimes with a situation (like sickness or hard storms), people don't know how to approach you, they don't know what to say, they don't know what to do. We don't really need pity. Nobody wants a pity party; we want strong people with strong faith!

And yes, I understand that people want to know that you're okay, but they tend to project their sadness onto you, so you have to be mindful to guard your ears, your eyes, your heart, and your spirit. The fire that God is putting you through may break them, but it is making you.

I know beyond a doubt that this is just a chapter in my story, its apart of my journey and there are people that I have invited along the way to share the journey with me, but I don't want to have people feeling sorry me! Nope we are not doing that. I am full of gratitude. I am gracious. I am grateful. I am hopeful.

When the storms in life are raging, you don't always want to be reminded of how things are going wrong, you truly need to be able to feel normal and that is what the branches in our lives help us do- they keep us steady. Get some people around you that can speak healing with you, believe God for you, and keep you up-lifted when life is at its darkest.

This is why we celebrate the beauty behind the scars, because not everything that happens to us during our seasons of testing is all bad. God is always working everything out for our good, including exposing the weaknesses in relationships of people and continually showing us who is really there.

I believe that God only wants the best for you and me, the best doctors, parents, teams, people etc., and we have to trust Him as we are going through dark times. We are not people who don't know who our God is – no we are not orphans. We have a great father and an entire camp of angels surrounding us waiting to hear our words of how we view our situation.

My mom can't do this for me. If my sister was here, I know she would try to speak faith for me, I know my dad would too. But no, this is my storm and I have to speak to my storm and be the boss of it and tell it where to go and what to do. You and I are not just living for the generations that we have here. No! I want my children's children to know that we faced a giant in this family but in our blood line, we win because we speak faith.

I know that God will keep me on the mind of the doctors and that he will guide them as they make every incision according to His will, and they will find that the cancer has not traveled to any other place. In faith I also declare that I will not have any adverse reactions to the surgery.

We know your son Jesus was wounded for our transgressions and by his stripes we are healed. So, I call forth healing. I call forth every seed that has been sown on my behalf I ask that you bless them as they sow into a blessed vessel. God, I thank you. I glorify you. I thank you. IT IS WELL.

CHAPTER 6

Can You Stand the Cutting?

THE TIME HAS ARRIVED, SURGERY IS HERE. I'm sure if we all could predict the exact day we would be cut by the storms of life; we would prepare for them like I have to do with this fasting and prep for my surgery or try to prevent storms from happening all together.

But no, we can't do that, we can't prevent the storms of life from cutting us. What does it mean to have life cut you? I didn't mention this earlier that the final definition of a scar is, "a lasting moral or emotional injury."

These wounds and injuries can look be the disappointments of a bad health report, failures in relationships, your finances not being enough to carry you through a season. Divorce, losing a child, losing a loved one, getting into a bad car accident– we have not been promised a life full of happy days. In fact, Jesus said himself, "In this world you will have trouble but take heart, I have overcome the world." John 16:33 NIV. Yes, all of us are walking around with some sort of physical, mental, or emotional scars we have all gone through a hard fight.

Your scars are symbolism of the fact that you have had to overcome your battle and how you tell the story, all depends on the way that you look at those scars and if you see the beauty and representation of what you went through. You need to be reminded often that you can fight, and that you are a warrior. When women have babies and get a c-section they come out with scars and there is so much beauty in that. As women we are so beautiful, and so many women cover their scars, find beauty products to make the scars disappear, or take makeup and smooth over the rough areas.

On the cover of this book I chose to proudly display my scars. I knew that people would have something to say about it, but I don't care. I want you to know that with your scars there is nothing to fear, nothing to hate, nothing to hide.

Our scars remind us that we are warriors who have survived every single bad day that the enemy has thrown our way. Our scars are symbols of hope, survival, they tell the story that God has won AGAIN!

During my prep for surgery I had to have radiation, and a mix of several medicines. My nurse said it would feel like a few glasses of wine and as sure as Peachtree goes to Buckhead, it felt like I had the whole bottle, ha but God was with me. I felt him with me, even with the smallest of confirmations.

One of the confirmations was having the radiation nurse tech Cheri spell her name exactly like my middle name, two she was a woman of faith and three, she told me to come back and see her in two years when I have my baby! God just kept letting me know that he is was me. I remember saying to my mamma, "Next time you see me my lovely breasts will not be there, but neither will cancer!"

What you lose in the battle will never compare to the peace and victory that you will gain. Many times, we lose focus in the battle and allow the enemy to win, simply because we spend so much time focusing on what we are going to lose or have lost. Losing does not mean that you are a failure. Losing does not mean that you are broken beyond repair. Losing does not mean that God has not moved. Losing important pieces of you, like how I am losing my breasts, simply means that you give up what is temporarily holding you back for something far greater – like your health, your life, your strength.

I am reminded of this meme I keep seeing on social media, where this little girl is holding onto a very small teddy bear, but Jesus is standing in front of her with a much bigger bear behind his back. He was pushing her to let go of that smaller bear first, so that he could bless her with something bigger that what she imagined.

Many of us are like that little girl, holding onto that small bear thinking that God couldn't possibly bless us with something extra- something more. We have to give up what we think is bringing us comfort, in order for God to work his real miracles.

If I had not let go of these breasts by getting a mastectomy, I would have never had a chance to experience God as a healer.

****

My surgery went well, and I was really sore and uncomfortable which was to be expected. As soon as I was able to realize where I was, one of my best friends sent me a picture of a rainbow just outside of the hospital- no let me rephrase, God sent me a rainbow to remind me of his promise, just like he is reminding you.

When I finally saw my breasts after surgery yes, I cried. They didn't look as bad as I thought and there were tears because I didn't expect them to look like they did. They were severely bruised, but they are my battle scars. I had to have my drains in, my pain medicine close by and my mother of course by my side helping me with every single thing I need. I could not have asked for a better tribe.

I am grateful to have people around me that know God for themselves who have a prayer life that they aren't afraid to pray with you and for you when you need them the most. Four days after my surgery, I found out that my prayers and my faith walk to not have chemo was answered- there is no trace that cancer has traveled in my body.

You heard me right, I am completely healed from cancer! I was able to truly praise God in the shower no matter how much it hurt. We bombarded heaven and God heard, not that I ever doubted, but I didn't know how this part of the story would go. I was faithful and hopeful that it would go this way.

• CHAPTER 7 •

The Healing Process

IN MY DAYS POST-SURGERY, I EXPERIENCED SO MANY UPS AND DOWNS, BUT I KNOW THIS IS TO BE EXPECTED. Recovering is funny because it is the simple things that you miss, not the big things. I have learned so many things about my body and how it responds to healing. There was a lot of rest in the midst of soreness, like two cement blocks were sitting on my chest, but all was well. All I could do was continue to trust and believe God and hold my faith high as I recovered through the healing process.

I have experienced nights where I could not go to sleep and not get in a comfortable position to lay in. I was grateful for the recovery pillows, but I did miss lying down on my side and on my tummy. I also accidently yanked my drains one night and that was beyond painful. I ended up eating too much on one particular night and while the food was delicious, my body quickly reminded me that I could not handle that!

Secondly, I have also learned in the healing process that you really need to give yourself time and rest. Our bodies are meant to heal themselves, but they are not magic- and neither are our spirits. I decided to resume some of my regular activities, like going back to church and having company over, but my mamma fussed at me that I was jumping back in too soon. I had to learn that rest was essential to recovery, no matter where I wanted to go. When you go through a hard battle, you need time to rest in your recovery process.

Finally, though, the day came during my recovery that I was able to get my drains out and become more mobile. I had no idea how much of a relief those little plastic tubes coming out would be. During this process I had to learn how to get myself out of bed, wash myself, get dressed and sleep without the full ability to move my arm and shower. But with my momma helping me like a little kid again, I was able to get everything I needed accomplished. Hey, I even have a little side boob that I am grateful to see -ha ha.

****

Listen I know recovery is hard, sometimes recovery and healing can be a worse pain than the cutting caused. You are forced to relive the moments, tell people that you truly need help and can't make it on your own, and you have to rest at the time you want to work.

One of the strategies that God gave me to help with our healing is to sow seed in faith and be sure to tell our seed where we want it to go. God is a god of covenant and I believe that when we sow, God does open up the windows of heaven on our behalf.

The day before my diagnosis, I made a large purchase (a generous seed) into the life of one of my leaders for their birthday. I didn't know I was going to hear that news but, I know my seed covered me. Then last year on Father's Day I helped with a large fee and two days later my`` sister passed. I can remember during that time having so much peace. Sowing seed is a faith move that is not for the faint at heart. I know, people think, "Oh, I'm not giving the church my money or I'm not giving them a monthly tithe," I get it, that's human nature but it's so much bigger than that. If a millionaire said to come and learn from them and it would cost a fee, but the goal was to learn so that you could have more money, you would do it right? So why do we think we can shortchange God when it comes to giving?

Sowing seeds is not only when you get a financial return but you receive blessings in so many other areas; The Lord can bless with you super natural strength, send divine help, opening the door for healing to happen (like catching your sickness in the early phases) he can even provide protection for my children's children, your marriage, spouse, your future. We sow in faith because the principal of reaping and sowing ensures us blessings. Do not forget to sow as you are healing. Give God your very best so that he can stand by his end of the covenant.

Another strategy I have learned is that our bodies need a great amount of water to recover. Bear with me friend, I am going somewhere with this water thing. In the bible, The Word of God can be compared to The Living Water and if our physical bodies can shut down and not heal properly with only giving it small amounts of water, imagine what not drinking in the word of God is doing to our spirits! Some of us can't get through hard storms because we are spiritually dehydrated.

To help you really boss your healing process, boss your boobies, and celebrate the beauty behind your scars, I have below a little cheat sheet if you will of the word of God to use when your faith is under attack:

1. Now to him who is able to do immeasurably more than all we ask or imagine, according to his power that is at work within us. — Ephesians 3:20

2. For God has not given us the spirit of fear; but of power, and of love, and of a sound mind- 2 Timothy 1:7

3. "LORD my God, I called to you for help, and you healed me." — Psalm 30:2

Listen I could go on and on finding scriptures, there are so many promises in The Word of God about our healing there is not enough room to record them all!

CHAPTER 8

Loving Your Body Again

ENJOYING LIFE AGAIN INSIDE YOUR BODY WHEN YOU HAVE FELT VIOLATED BY SICKNESS OR PAIN CAN BE A VERY VULNERABLE THING. You wonder if you will ever feel or be normal? You wonder if your body will betray you again, or if you can predict if something is going to happen in the future so that your circumstances won't be that bad.

In one of our recent church services we focused on prophesying to yourself. I am so grateful that God has given me the gift of FAITH, not just having faith but the gift where I can believe God for anything. Many years ago, my Bishop preached about how your words create your world. A series that literally changed my life. Changed how I viewed things and in turn the words that I speak which I believe has helped me increase my faith. It is amazing to be able to speak those things that be not as though they were and believe that those things will come to pass. Even in this I will continue to speak that my body is free of ALL CANCER!! And it will continue to be!

Our faith indeed needs to have the final say, and it's so important for us as women in particular to love the bodies that god has given us and be confident inside of them. We have been fearfully and wonderfully made and we truly are a reflection of the beauty God created. I don't like it when I hear women who hate their bodies, or certain parts of us that we want to disappear, be smaller, or wish wasn't there. I definitely feel like it's okay to make enhancements to your body if you want to, but we should not give the enemy permission to torment us, comparing ourselves to someone else's body thinking we look worse. No!

You have been made after God's image and in his likeness. God did not make a mistake with you and you should fight to enjoy life inside of your body. While we are here on earth, this is the only body we will get. I wish every time our bodies messed up, we could just turn it in and get a new one like a car, but this is the only body we receive.

We will face challenges inside these bodies, but we have to learn to love this casing that we are in. So, in case you haven't had a momma like mine to remind you that no matter your scars that you are still beautiful, hear it from me speaking directly to you: YOU ARE BEAUTIFUL! SCARS AND ALL!

Your mind is beautiful, your soul is beautiful, your heart is beautiful, your body is beautiful. This world would not be the same without you here. You have wonderful gifts to bring the world and a testimony to share. Don't you dare let anything keep you silent.

That is what the enemy wants from you. He wants you to be so broken and to hate yourself so much that you can't open your mouth and say anything positive about yourself, God, or others! You deserve more than that; you have a price far above rubies.

When something as serious as breast cancer comes knocking at your door, you allow the word of God to answer and to be your response. Anticipating rejection and fearing so much about what people think ends here. We have to know that we are beautiful no matter what and that our scars have purpose.

You are not on this earth by accident, you have a divine purpose for being here in this time, moment, this year to let someone else know that they can make it. This book is just one of the ways that I am letting the world know that my God is faithful and that there is purpose in the pain that we go through.

So, think about your scars- from the deep ones to the shallow ones – what story do you have to tell? What words are you speaking in faith to create an atmosphere for God to move? No more looking at your scars and your past in shame, always know there is beauty behind your scars!

Father I thank you for the woman of God or man of God reading this story. I thank you that they no longer see themselves as small but that they boss their faith and know that you are with them no matter what. You have given them so much beauty behind their scars and we pray for every stronghold to be broken so that they can live in freedom! With joy unspeakable! I know God that you are able to deliver them and keep them no matter what storms they face! I thank you for surrounding them with the right people and that they will guard their ear gates and eye gates against hearing things that are opposite to your word and seeing negative things that are opposite to your word. I thank you that in their darkest nights and hours you remind them that you are with them and that you said you would never leave them nor forsake them. I thank you that you have given them a story to tell and that they won't be ashamed of that story, but that they walk in confidence knowing no weapon formed against them will be able to prosper! In Jesus name we pray,

Amen!

-   Latisia Jones

About Latisia Jones

Breast cancer survivor and Atlanta, GA native Latisia Jones, affectionately known by her brand as The Educated Boss Chic, is a servant leader, teacher, and breast cancer early screening advocate.

She is a respected leader at New Faith Christian Church, holding the position as Chief Armor Bearer to the Co-Pastor, Lady Laurona Phelps primary assistant to the first family.

As a solid educator with 14 years of experience in middle grades, Ms. Jones has a unique ability to capture, cultivate and nurture the minds of our future. She is also an advocate for her fellow educators to boss their health, faith, and finances.

She has earned her bachelor's degree in English, a Master's in Education, and a Specialist degree in Curriculum and Instruction.

****

For booking, speaking, apparel and more visit:

www.theeducatedbosschic.com

WORKS CITED

- PAGE 11 - 2 TIMOTHY 1:7.

- PAGE 17- John 16:33 NIV.
- PAGE 42- "Though he slay me, yet will I trust," Job 13:15

PAGE 16- AMERICAN CANCER SOCIETY CANCER FACTS 2019 www.theamericancancersociety.com.https://www.cancer.org/content/dam/cancer-org/research/cancer-facts-and-statistics/cancer-facts-and-figures-for-african-americans/cancer-facts-and-figures-for-african-americans-2019-2021.pdf .

- Black women are not taking action. While 92% of black women agree breast health is important, only 25% have recently discussed breast health with their family, friends, or colleagues. And, only 17% have taken steps to understand their risk for breast cancer.
- Black Women are often at a more advanced stage upon detection.
- Black women may not have access to health care or health insurance so may have lower frequency of longer intervals between mammograms.

- Because they may not have insurance, Black women may not follow up on abnormal mammogram results because they can't afford the diagnostic testing.
- Black women don't get the same prompt high quality treatment compared to white women.
- Black women have the highest odds (2 times more likely) of getting Triple Negative Breast Cancer, a kind of breast cancer that often is aggressive and comes back after treatment. It has the highest mortality rate and is the only breast cancer sub-type that does not have a therapy to prevent recurrence. Note that younger women and women diagnosed at later stages arc more likely to get Triple Negative Breast Cancer.